BUILDING A BUSINESS PLAN:
FEATURING BUSINESS PLAN PRO SOFTWARE

David E. Tooch
University of New Hampshire, Thompson School

Pearson
Education

Upper Saddle River, New Jersey 07458

Acquisitions editor: David Parker
Assistant editor: Ashley Keim
Production editor: Carol Zaino
Cover Printer: Phoenix Color
Bindery/Text Manufacturer: Von Hoffman Graphics/MD

ISBN 0-13-100800-5

10 9 8 7 6 5 4 3 2 1

Table of Contents

Preface

The purpose and goal of this book is to turn your dreams into reality. This book provides a step-by-step guide to building a professional Business Plan.

A Business Plan is a documented formal proposal for:

- **The start-up of a new business venture**
- **The growth and expansion of an existing business**
- **The implementation of special projects such as:**

  - **In-house personnel programs**
  - **Marketing and sales proposals**
  - **Social cause ventures**
  - **Government legislation**
  - **Special funding requests**
  - **Non-profit organization functions**
  - **Export programs**
  - **And many more**

A Business Plan serves as:

- **Your application for the required permits, licenses and approvals.**
- **Your application for financing.**
- **Your confirmation of the likelihood of success.**
- **Your plan to follow for the first 12-24 months of operation.**

This book uses a selection of actual client cases that follows the logical sequence and process for building a Business Plan. Each chapter includes a related student activity that allows you to build your plan in an easy-to-follow step-by-step process. This format serves to transform a seemingly overwhelming task into a series of focused steps that stand on their own and require a relatively short time to complete.

In addition to full subject matter coverage, the final chapter is dedicated to professional presentation aspects of your finished product. Appearance and first impressions, professional writing and presentation are everything in today's business world.

Options for Your Unique Business Plan

This book is designed as both a stand-alone guide to building your business plan and as a supplement to Palo Alto Software's **Business Plan Pro**-- a user-friendly cd that also works with you to create your business plan.

We recommend that you use both products. This combination will provide you with the widest range of topics, format options and opportunities available in order to build your very best business plan.

The software product features:

- Spreadsheets with column and row headings-- you just fill in the blanks.
- Pie Charts and Graphs-- you just fill in the variables.
- Standard blocks of business text-- you may choose to use a variety for your plan.
- Outside references and readings-- easy access to relevant data and information.
- Samples of actual business plans.

This book features:

- A complete outline, action plan and time line for building your business plan.
- Actual case studies and results that explain and illustrate each component of a business plan.
- Case related student activities that help you build your unique plan, step by step.
- Insights, strategies and classroom opportunity teaching notes for your instructor.

You will discover similarities and differences in the subject matter and topical coverage of both business plan building products. This gives you a great opportunity to pick and choose from each as you work through the process of building your unique business plan. And thanks to the flexibility of each product, you have the choice of attaching word documents from the book to the software and/or attaching software documents to the book.

The student activity section of each chapter concludes with a boxed **"BPPRO SIDEBAR"** that makes it easy for you to either attach your word document to the software or to access and complete the specific section of the software and download those documents to the book.

Your instructor's expectations and guidelines will help to bring it all together in a productive and successful fashion.

Tip for Success

- Peruse the book before you begin, paying special attention to the student activity sections and requirements. Peruse the software package as well. As you click your way through the table of contents, take the time to look at any of those section headings that are unfamiliar to you.

- Keep in mind that you will have the opportunity to collect data for more than one section at a time as you conduct your fieldwork and research. For example, your analysis of the competition will provide the opportunity to take notes on personnel management, location and layout options and variables.

- Your overview of the contents of each resource will set you up nicely for a smooth transition into your chapter 1 student activity which requires you to select your business, to draft both an executive summary and business description, and to create an outline and action plan.

- Take advantage of the best of both worlds. Take advantage of the presence and guidance of your instructor. Cut and paste your way to an exciting experience and to your best, most complete and professional business plan.

About the Author

David E. Tooch grew up working in a successful family business and continued on to experience a wide range of positions ranging from soldier to laborer, top manager and business owner. Tooch has worked in the hospitality field, in retail, in the NYC garment district, the forest products industry and in education and government throughout the United States.

Tooch holds two undergraduate degrees in natural resource management and a masters degree in business. Tooch is currently Associate Professor of Business at The University of New Hampshire's Thompson School, and also serves as Consultant, Trainer, Speaker and Writer for industries and associations nationwide. He has published more than 120 articles on management applications, and is the author of three books.

Tooch's trademark is industry proven, hands-on applications that get results.

Comments and inquiries are always welcomed. Tooch may be reached at P.O. Box 147, Durham, New Hampshire, USA 03824, det@cisunixunh.edu and (603) 862-1195.

Author's Thanks

Just a little bit of space and time to sincerely thank the following:

- David Parker, Prentice Hall Acquisitions Editor for his belief in and support of my hands-on teaching methodology and vision of the marketplace

- Steve Deitmer, Prentice Hall Editor for his outstanding use and knowledge of the language and related editorial contributions

- Tim Berry, President of Palo Alto Software for his generosity and help in connecting this book to his fine software products

CHAPTER 1

The Business Plan: Introduction, Sample Case & General Outline

What, Why, How, for Whom

A privately owned business is a part of the spirit of America. The right and privilege of "being your own boss" and "building your own empire" is an ingredient of our country's freedom and success.

Suppose that you, or you and a partner, or a group of you, want to buy or build a new business. Where do you begin? How do you actually do it? It almost always begins with the creation of a Business Plan.

A Business Plan is a document where "it" all comes together. "It", in this case, is made up of: a statement or explanation of exactly what your business is, a description of your niche in the market, an explanation of why your business will be an asset to the community and to the economy in general, a description of your location and facilities, a verification of the financial feasibility of your venture, a look at your administration, and a place where the answers to various agency's and people's questions may be found.

A Business Plan distinguishes a pipedream from a reality. Is your business venture destined for success or doomed for failure? If the initial proposal does not look promising, this is not necessarily the end. It may mean you have to revise your plan to include new or more diverse markets, or other changes to get you over the top.

Once all of the particulars are in place, the Business Plan becomes a map to follow, at least for the first year or two of operation.

Creating a Business Plan is not difficult. It is time-consuming, but it is mostly just a collection of information. In the "real world", it may take upwards of a year or more to complete, so your instructor may modify some of the specific requirements to fit your schedule and/or to fit the mission of your class. The most important thing is for you to work through the process. Once you have done that, you will have a foundation of knowledge and experience that can pay off many times in many ways throughout your entire career.

A new business venture usually requires the support and cooperation of many institutions and individuals. You may be surprised to learn that the first question these organizations and their people may ask is, "Let's see your Business Plan" Once the final draft is in place (a business venture destined for success), you will have a document that serves as a financing proposal for banks and other investors and a document that supports your requests for the various permits and approvals that may be required.

Sample Case

Scott Mac is a business student. His parents have owned a small tennis club near Chicago for many years. The club has a limited exercise and fitness room, a locker room, and a small pro shop and snack bar. The facility, in a great location, sits on a spacious lot with room to grow.

Scott has always been a working member of the family business, and it is the entrepreneurial spirit of his parents that inspired him to want to be his own boss and to attend a business school for some basic training. A business thinker with vision, he has many ideas for new products and services. He is nearing the completion of his schooling, and is anxious to return to the business and to put his ideas into action.

Scot has learned that the country's #1 ranked growth industry is the health sector. This area includes fitness, nutrition, and leisure management, as well as the more traditional health services.

The tennis club is the "retirement policy" for Scott's parents, who have worked hard for twenty-four years, building the business from scratch. They want to receive the club's asset value and a fair return on investment for the club's goodwill – that is, the name and reputation they have developed over the years. The family has learned that the local banks will finance only 70%-80% of the value of the fixed assets of the business (land, buildings and equipment). Scott has saved about $100,000, but knows that this is not enough. In fact, Scott's parents want to see a formal Business Plan.

Actual Results

Scott began by studying the table of contents options for the **Business Plan Pro** software, and the attached Exhibit 1: Outline/Guideline for the Creation of a Business Plan. Scott also spent some time brainstorming with his classmates, professors, and parents. It became apparent that he could not begin his Business Plan without the creation of an Executive Summary, also known as a Business Description. This item may include, but is not limited to:

- A Description of the Business
- Company Mission Statement
- Short- Term and Long-Term Goals
- Location and Facilities
- Products and Services
- Keys to Success
- Start-up Summary

Scott drew up the following Executive Summary:

The Mac Tennis Club has served the local community for twenty-four years. To meet the demands of its loyal customer base and of the many new members of its growing community, plans call for a major expansion of the currently facility and the addition of the Mac's son Scott as managing partner. The tennis facilities and related products and services will continue to be offered in the great tradition established and developed by the Mac family.

Plans call for a 60,000-square-foot addition to the existing building that will include one additional tennis court, four racquetball courts, a fitness equipment room, two exercise studios, an indoor track, and an expanded locker room, pro shop and food court.

The current location meets all of the local commercial zoning laws and regulations, and includes adequate space for the building addition, expanded parking, and other related facilities and maintenance needs.

The addition of a fitness trainer and registered diet technician will allow for increased health and wellness services. The expanded food court will offer full-service breakfast, lunch and dinner each day. A banquet/function room will accommodate private parties of up to forty.

Short-term goals call for the completion of the project within eighteen months. Current tennis and related products and services will not be affected by the construction. The new facility will be designed and built to allow for any future changes needed to meet longer-term market needs and demands.

Keys to success include a continuation of the already well-established products, services and traditions of the Mac family, the introduction of new products and services that the local community demands, a solid financial base from which to operate, and strong support from the local community and from the club's many long-term employees.

*   *   *

The Executive Summary can be written and presented in many forms. But its major goal is to establish a clear focus, benchmark, and point of reference for the Business Plan research.

Scott's final step in preparing his Business Plan research is his action plan/outline and timeline, which can be easily set up by using the attached Exhibit 1 Guideline and/or the **Business Plan Pro** table of contents options. Note once again how the Executive Summary and/or Business Description serve as the benchmark and point of reference for all subsequent research.

EXHIBIT 1

Guideline for the Creation of a Business Plan

Executive Summary (typically one page): Any reader can clearly see what they are about to read, what your methodology was, what the major contents of the piece are, your final conclusions, and a reference to supporting documentation.

Major categories:

- Description of Business: Products, services, location, mission, short- and long-term goals.

- Market Research/Data, Analysis, and Conclusion: a well-written summary narrative of your analysis of the competition and analysis of the customer base, ultimately leading to your sales forecast for the first two years of operation (see Appendix 1).

- Approvals, Permits, Licenses: verification that all of the necessary approvals and permits have been obtained from the appropriate city/town, state, and federal agencies (see Appendix 2).

- Financial Data: A summary narrative, and: sources and uses statement, projected income statements, cash flow statements, and balance sheets for the first two years of operation (see Appendix 3).

- Organization and Staffing: organizational chart with job titles and job descriptions for each staff member, along with credentials/resumes of management team, and operating procedures (see Appendix 4).

- Other: includes information unique and relevant to your situation-- for example, franchise information, equipment and supplier information, contracts, real estate data, and so on. (see Appendix 5).

Appendices (Include separate folders/files for each):

- Appendix 1: Notes, observations, interviews, and other data from analysis of competition and customer base that led to your sales forecast.
- Appendix 2: Appropriate (sample) forms.
- Appendix 3: Supporting documentation to financials.
- Appendix 4: Appropriate and relevant data.
- Appendix 5: As necessary

<u>Week 1 Student Activity</u>

The Business Plan Connection

Congratulations! You are about to learn how to research and write a business plan. Whether you ever actually own your own business or not, this process and the resulting documentation have far-reaching effects. You may want to buy or build a home someday, create and lead a special project at work, promote a cause, or complete a community service project. In each instance, a business plan will help you establish specific goals and achieve your desired results.

There are three steps for you to take to get started:

1. **Select a Business**. For some of you, this is easy, because you already know what you want to do. For others, it is a more difficult decision, but you must choose something. What occupation or industry are you most interested in at this moment? If the genie came out of the bottle and offered you any job in the world, what would you choose? Do your parents or some other close family member or friend own a business? What about your current job? If the decision is still not easy, take some more time to think about it, but be sure to select something that you have an interest in, which will make drawing up the business plan much more interesting and fun.

2. **Establish a Specific Focus**. Begin with the Business Description. Describe the business, its location, and its products and services. What are the primary markets that it will serve? What about its legal form of ownership, the layout of the facilities, and the number of employees? Sufficient detail and a clear focus up front will make this project easier to complete.

3. **Outline your Action Plan**: Given the amount of time that you have, and the specific requirements of your instructor, map out a weekly plan of action. What will you accomplish this week, next week, and the week after? The majority of your time will be spent collecting information, observing and interviewing. Be sure to leave a week or two at the end of the project for preparing your written plan and formally presenting it.

Tips for Success

- Refer to the table of contents options from this book, from the **Business Plan Pro** software and from Exhibit 1. These will help you set up your outline and focus, your time line and your action plan.

- Expect change as you go. Though some people will follow their plan through exactly as written, you may discover that a change in plans is necessary as you collect information, make observations, and shift your focus.

- What's most important at this time is to select your business, describe it, and create a plan of action.

BPPRO SIDEBAR

The Business Plan Pro includes 400+ sample business plans. Install BPPro, run it on your computer, and start a business plan. Use the "Sample Plan" icon on the toolbar to find one of the sample plans that interests you. Use the command in the Sample Plan browser File menu to load that plan into BPPro. While you are looking at that plan, click the "Plan Outline" tool on the toolbar to access the outline view. Click on the Table of Contents to show a form that lets you print the Table of Contents.

Take a close look at the section headings and subcategories, from section 1.0 to the end, paying special attention to both the similarities and differences between this document and the table of contents and exhibit 1 categories from this book. Now think about the particulars of your own unique business plan. Which of the three lists matches up best? Are you more inclined to build your plan using the book approach (word documents with software attachments) or the software approach (BPPro applications with word document attachments)? You may discover that this is your first opportunity to take advantage of the best of both worlds by creating your own unique table of contents that uses headings and subcategories from both products.

BPPro includes a great deal of flexibility to adjust an outline to your exact needs. Just to make sure you can, delete a topic (choose any topic anywhere within the outline), and then, after leaving that topic out of the plan, add it back in. Then add an entirely new topic, anywhere in the outline. Save the sample plan as a copy on your hard disk, using the BPPro "Save As" command. Be sure to give it a relevant file name that you will remember.

Now either start a new plan or open the plan you saved earlier. Find the SIC code (standard industry code system) section of the Plan Setup step in the Plan Wizard (hint: if you left your BPPro in the Plan Outline mode for the last exercise, you'll need to click the "Wizard Tasks" icon to see the Plan Setup steps. If your plan started from a sample plan, with its SIC code already identified, write that SIC number down where you'll be able to find it later).

Now experiment with the sample plan browser and the SIC code searcher to explore different types of businesses. Using the sample plan browser, choose three sample plans from the list, one each for SIC codes starting with 5, 6, and 7. Write down the names of the three sample plans you chose, because you will use them later.

CHAPTER 2

Case Study: The Witches Brew: A New Business Venture;

The Approval Process: Will you be allowed to do what you want to do?

Introduction

Paul, Steve, and Jen graduated from a local business college several years back and have kept in close touch. They plan to form a partnership to fulfill a lifetime dream of establishing a micro-brewery and restaurant, which they will call the Witches Brew. Paul has spent the past five years training to become a master brewer. Both Steve and Jen have worked in several area restaurants, working their way into management positions. They have located the "perfect" building and have sufficient funds for the down payment, with enough left over to serve as start-up working capital.

The building, completed around 1851, is a former stone church near the busy waterfront shopping area of Portsmouth New Hampshire. That section of the city is currently zoned for residential use only, but the building is right on the border of the commercially zoned waterfront district. They plan to serve food and drink both indoors and out, and the property includes 200 feet of waterfront, which if developed would accommodate their plans for boat access and waterside service. A portion of the land abutting the water is classified as "wetlands".

Their plans call for a glass atrium extension to the existing building, which would provide increased seating capacity. The site would be considered a manufacturing facility as well as a retail/service business because six large beer vats will be in various stages of the brewing process. These vats would continuously service customers. There is a question concerning the volume of water usage as well as the disposal of the waste from the manufacturing process. The property falls within the boundary of city water and sewer service.

There is a second floor that would be used for catered functions and for overflow restaurant service. There is plenty of parking, but currently no handicapped access to either the main building or second floor. The property sits on a state road that runs through the city.

An Overview of the Approval Process

Up until ten or twenty years ago, depending on your particular location in the country, the first and only real question to answer regarding the likelihood of success for any new business venture was the market. Would there be enough demand to generate the level of sales necessary for desired profits? If the answer to this question was no, the story ended, or you at least went back to the drawing board to revise plans. If the answer was yes, the project might be a go, and everything else (operations, overhead, and so on) would tend to fall into place. This answer was and still is a function of the level and degree of competition in the area and of the spending power and buying behavior of the customer base and target markets.

Since that time, the approval process has gained equal importance to the market question in many areas of the country, and so has become the "second first-step" of the business plan building process.

This change results from a combination of increased population density and growth, related traffic issues, police/fire/safety concerns; demand for city services such as schools, roads, and waste removal; environmental issues, legal issues, real estate value and appreciation, moral issues, politics, and other variables related to the "public good".

While it is unlikely that anyone would ever have to address all of these issues, it is also unlikely that a business venture would just move along without having to overcome a few of these challenges.

We use the term "approval process" described in this case, as a catch-all phrase for the various permits, licenses, certificates, fees, and board approvals that may be required to move along with business plans including any and all of the local, state, and federal agencies that may come into play.

The other approval process factors to consider are time and cost. Depending on the particular business and location, it may take anywhere from six-months to eighteen-months and many thousands of dollars just to be allowed to move forward with your business plans.

Issues and Questions Relevant to This Case

While Portsmouth, New Hampshire, happens to be a pro-growth city, the city council wants to see a business plan. These elected board members are responsible for the welfare of the city and its people. Their job is to ensure that any new business will be a true asset to the community. They are concerned about the impact on, and demand for city services, jobs and employment, safety and environmental issues. How should these concerns be addressed?

The principles- Paul, Steve, and Jen-- wish to establish a commercial venture in a section of town zoned for residential use. Does the zoning need to be changed, or can a variance or special exception be granted? Any such change requires a formal application to modify the rules on a one-time basis due to extraordinary or extenuating circumstances. This process also requires supporting documentation and justification. What is the best way to approach this situation and these appointed town officials?

Portsmouth, like many communities deep in the heart of New England have a Historical Society whose mission is to maintain the historical perspective and integrity of the city. Will this local group of citizens approve of the plans for the Witches Brew? Does this group have any power or authority?

The State Division of Environmental Services works with the local Conservation Commission regarding the development of wetland sites and other environmentally sensitive proposals. This group also plays a role in processing permits. Will the wetlands be an issue? Will the Coast Guard and/or Port Authority need to be involved given the plans for pier access and dockside services?

Then there is the question of the large volume of water required for making the beer and the waste the process generates. Will special permits or provisions be required? Is an environmental impact statement necessary?

Does the city have a building inspector? Is a building permit required? What specifications must be met? Do these specifications include state and federal requirements issued by OSHA, the Department of Energy, and so on?

This proposed venture is located on a state road. Although the city may approve the project, the state may not, depending on the impact on traffic flow and safety. Who would be responsible for any road renovations that may be required?

How difficult, expensive, and time-consuming is it to obtain a food and liquor license? What about handicapped accessibility? Will it be necessary to install special ramps and/or elevators? Is there anything else we're forgetting?

The Intangibles

Most of the questions we've considered so far are "black-and-white". Either you need a permit or you don't, and if you do, the process to get one is straight-forward. There are however issues of politics, attitudes, and personalities.

While you may have a hard time getting anyone to admit to this, the fact is that certain people with certain attitudes and agendas, have the authority to say yes or no to a proposal. They also have the ability to create significant roadblocks and additional costs.

Is the town in question pro-growth or no-growth? Do the town leaders want you operating this type of business in their town? What is the current local unemployment rate? Are you promising new jobs for local people?

Might unemployment, development, or other issues make your business proposal attractive? Are there opportunities for tax incentives, low-rate financing, labor cost-share, or special lease arrangements? It is certainly in your best interest to find out.

Paul, Steve, and Jen- the principles-- have signed a purchase and sales agreement for the property, contingent on receiving the necessary permits and approvals and on securing the necessary financing. The closing is set for 90 days from now, with an option for an extension with the written agreement of both parties. But the owners want to sell within a reasonable amount of time. They plan to use the money to build a new and much larger church in another part of town.

Actual Results of Case

Following a careful review of the business plan, the City Council referred the principles to the Zoning Board of Adjustment, which granted a 'special exception permit' allowing for commercial use of a residentially zoned property. This process alone took three months, and required certified letters to all property abutters, a public hearing, and the hiring of a local surveying and engineering firm, which prepared and presented the necessary maps and plot plans and answered questions regarding environmental and other development concerns.

The engineering firm also addressed all questions and issues raised about the use of city water and disposal of manufacturing waste. No specific permits were required. The principles will simply pay the going rate for water usage.

The city's Port Authority issued the necessary permits for boat access, landing and mooring.

The atrium addition proposal was dropped because of strong opposition from the local historical society, which determined it to not be in keeping with the historical perspective and integrity of the downtown waterfront district. The principles chose not to fight that battle after consulting with their attorney.

The Division of Environmental Services permits were obtained for wetlands development and for dock/pier construction and access. The conditions of the permit were strict but reasonable. This process also took three months and required a presentation at the monthly Conservation Commission meeting, an on-site inspection by that group along with its letter of support, and the necessary forms and fees submitted to the state Division of Environmental Services.

Portsmouth, a pro-growth town, wanted the business. The principles were escorted through the remaining approval/permit process rather quickly and easily (city council approval, building and occupancy permits).

The state issued liquor and food licenses with the understanding that employees would be trained and liability insurance obtained. The state highway department granted access to and from the state road that abuts the property. This step was easy thanks to the road improvements and landscaping that the church had paid for in years past. It would have been the responsibility of the principles to pay for any safety improvements to the state road.

Handicapped access was provided to both the main and second levels of the building and to the pier seating in accordance with federal mandates.

End Note

Paul, Steve, and Jen now find themselves happy and a bit overwhelmed. Their business plan, which took six months to prepare, helped to earn them permission to move ahead with their project. The approval process, which took six months and cost $12,000 is complete.

They are now set to move ahead with their market analysis summary and strategy and implementation summary (**Sections 3.0 and 4.0 Business Plan Pro Software**) and to secure the required financing should the market analysis turn out to be favorable.

Please note that the **Business Plan Pro Software** does not include an Approval Process section. These requirements will vary greatly depending on your specific location. Refer to the Week 2 Student Activity and the Business Plan Connection for further detail and direction.

WEEK 2 Student Activity

The Business Plan Connection

In your Week 1 Activity you created both a formal Business Plan Outline and a detailed Business Description. These pieces will serve as the benchmark or point of reference for your original draft of the Business Plan, which may or may not change depending on the results of your research. Your business description should have addressed the following:

- What specific business are you in?

- What specific products and services will you offer?

- What specific location have you chosen, and why?

With this information and knowledge in hand, it is now time for some web searches, phone calls, and in-person visits to the appropriate local, state, federal, and appropriate agencies.

Start with the **local town or city hall**. The people in charge will probably want to know if you are proposing to continue with the same business in the same location, with a new business in an existing location, or with a new business in a new location.

You should inquire about zoning, a building permit, planning board/city council approval and other local requirements. **Be sure to obtain a copy of any and all forms that need to be filled out.**

Local town or city halls almost always have staff members with many years experience who are very knowledgeable and helpful in these matters.

You will also learn a most valuable lesson during these inquiries and meetings. You will find that when properly approached, these people will guide you through the process, offering you information, pointing out do's and don'ts, and giving you the perspective of each approval/permit/board. They can really help you take the path of least resistance.

You are now ready to move on to the various **state and federal agencies** to collect additional information.

Next consider any **industry-specific** licenses or permits that you may need. If you are venturing into industries such as real estate, accounting/financial planning, hair styling, electrical/plumbing contracting, or practicing law, just to name a few, you will discover additional requirements such as a license, a test or certification, a certificate or degree, and so on.

Finally, after you make these inquiries, take notes, and collect sample forms, then piece together an estimate of the **amount of time and expense** that will be incurred. For example, a building project often begins with a land survey, a water and sewer design, and a building plan, all of which may take weeks or months, may cost several thousands of dollars, and must be completed and approved by licensed professionals.

This student activity concludes with **Appendix I: Approval Forms and Related Information.**

Your instructor will provide you with his or her specific requirements. As a class/semester assignment, you may not have the time to collect all of the necessary information (which may take several weeks or months in the real world).

The goal of this exercise is ensure that you understand the approval process, why it exists, and how to proceed through it.

Tips for Success

1. Where/how to begin: Visit, call, or click on to your town or city hall and ask about the permits and approvals required to start a business.

2. Be prepared to clearly explain what your business is and where it will be. This will help the people you ask direct you to the right people, places, forms and information.

3. Ask for or download copies of the relevant forms and information. These will be very educational for you, and should be included in the appendix of your report.

4. Ask questions. Most town or city halls have employees who have been around for a long time and who know how day-to-day business is conducted. These people are there to help.

5. Have fun.

BPPRO SIDEBAR

The permit and approval process category is not included in the software. If you discover that these requirements are necessary and relevant to your business plan venture, then you should complete this student activity on a word document in accordance with your instructor's guidelines.

Those of you using the Business Plan Pro should click the "Plan Outline" tool bar to access your table of contents and then select the most appropriate place to add this chapter's title (and word file) to your existing business plan setup. Use the "Save As" command and give it a related file name.

CHAPTER 3

Case Study: The Witches Brew, A New Business Venture:

Market Analysis and Strategy Implementation: Will there be enough demand to generate the desired level of sales and profits?

Introduction

With the necessary permits and approvals in hand, Paul, Steve, and Jen must now focus their attention on the market.

The ultimate goal of any market analysis is to create a sales forecast. You can accomplish this through a four-step process:

1. **Observe, interview and analyze your competition**: Who are your competitors? What are their strengths and weaknesses? How much competition is there? How will you position yourself to compete?

2. **Observe, interview and analyze your customer base**: What are the demographics, trends, relevant statistics and overall buying behaviors of the population within your selling radius?

3. **Define and more closely study the specific target market segments that you select**. After studying your competition and customer base, you must decide on and prioritize which specific markets and buying groups you will target. This group of market segments (typically two or three distinct groups such as retailers, industrial buyers, overseas buyers, individual local consumer groups, and so on) would represent and generate 80% to 100% of your total sales. Part of this decision is also based on your physical resources and limitations (land, buildings, equipment, inventory, personnel and finances). Or in other words, which markets and buying groups (outside sales) will match up best with your physical plant, materials/inventory, personnel and financial constraints (inside operations)?

4. **Convert this data into the sales forecast**, in both units of volume and dollars of sales for the first one- to three-years of operation.

The sales forecast is the starting point for all financial projections, for all personnel planning and staffing needs, for the layout and operations of the physical plant, and for the many details you'll need and decisions that you'll make as you complete the Business Plan. In other words, the sales forecast helps you determine what it will take in terms of money, materials, people and facilities to generate your projected sales and profits both initially and long-term.

The end result of this process (the sales forecast) is also the starting point for your promotional mix. After figuring out how much you'll sell, you can determine your budget and specific plans for advertising, promotion, public relations, and personal selling force.

This case refers directly to **Sections 3.0 and 4.0 of the Business Plan Pro Software**. With the Student Activity tied to this case you'll complete the market analysis and strategy implementation summary for your Business Plan.

Relevant Case Issues

Paul, Steve, and Jen know that there is an abundance of competition in the area. This competition ranges from fast food national chain restaurants to five-star gourmet specialty houses, to hotels, to every imaginable ethnic cuisine, along with the local long-standing mom-and-pop home-style diners.

Their six-month "spy mission" helped them to understand that they cannot be all things to all people, and that they must focus on specific groups of clientele, and on a specific group of products and services given their market, personal and business goals, and physical resources and constraints.

They found that the competition collectively serves breakfast, lunch, and dinner, seven days per week. Some competitors also provide catering and banquet facilities and services, happy hour programs, event nights, and seasonal and holiday specials. Some go after blue-collar workers, while others go after the upper-middle to upper-class professionals. Then there are the business and government markets. Some competitors go after specific age groups, such as senior citizens, families, young couples, singles, and kids. Some places deliver and some don't. Some places make their own desserts and baked goods, while others buy them. And then there is the very large tourist crowd that shows up from Memorial Day to Labor Day each year. How do we draw them in? And we can't forget about the locals, now can we? What about smokers, vegetarians, and other diners with special needs?

Beyond these concerns, the principles also observed many styles of atmosphere and decor. The competition offers a wide range of furniture, lighting, music, and privacy. The staffing also varied from high school and college kids to more seasoned, veteran hospitality workers.

The principles also took note of parking, outside signs and lighting, nearby stores, neighborhoods, restroom facilities, artwork and room decor, and traffic flow.

The more they looked, the more overwhelming it became. Just how should they set up their establishment?

The process of competition analysis-- which, by the way, should never end-- is aimed at staying current with the market and at trying to capture and use all of the great ideas and applications that are out there, while at the same time avoiding costly mistakes. This analysis is also a great way to get and keep a pulse on the market, as successful businesses are in tune with their clientele. Those planning a new business venture are working to set up "the perfect business", while those already in business are aiming to survive and thrive.

The partners rounded out their competition analysis by speaking with everyone possible at each location. This included employees, managers and owners. They learned a lot about customer service, employee relations and motivation, community relations, government regulations and dealing with banks and bankers.

Their focus now shifted to the customer base analysis. They began by drawing a circle on a map, with their establishment at the center. The radius was a line extending twenty miles out. The partners felt that the vast majority of their buying public would come from the 200,000 or so people who live within that circle. Their goal now was to learn about those people.

There are two major categories of customer base information-- (1) existing data and statistics, and (2) surveys.

Paul, Steve, and Jen visited the city and town halls, chambers of commerce, and registry of deeds offices of every town within their buying circle. They were amazed at the abundance of useful and (mostly) free information. They found population statistics and trends, marriage, birth and death rates, existing and new housing start data and pricing, income and occupation data and road and school construction plans. Their pile of data grew quite large.

In theory, it would be nice to survey or interview each of the 200,000 people within the working circle in order to discover each person's buying wants and needs, but they learned that this was not practical or affordable. Instead, the principles contracted the services of a local marketing firm which put together a survey and guided the principles in selecting 2,000 people to serve as a representative cross-section of the total population. The data gathered, the marketing firm assured them, would be statistically accurate and reliable.

The principles asked questions about how often people dined out, why they selected one establishment over another; what they wanted on the menu, what they liked to pay, and other aspects of dining out. The survey also included open-ended questions that allowed people to express opinions and ideas outside of the structured multiple-choice questions.

The survey and market analysis took six months and was done simultaneously with their approval and permit activities.

With competitor and customer analysis complete, the question for both the principles themselves and their prospective creditors stood before them: **would there be enough demand to generate the desired level of sales and profits?**

Actual Results of Case

Paul, Steve, and Jen were wise to solicit the opinions of several area professionals including the marketing firm that prepared and tabulated their survey, consultants from the Small Business Administration, and former business professors-- along with a few trusted friends and advisors. After hundreds of hours of hard work, data analysis and brainstorming sessions, they were able to document their specific market plan.

They decided to target two major local groups: (1) the 21- to 35-year-old single and married white-collar professionals, and (2) the 35- to 55-year-old middle- to upper-middle-class white-collar professionals. These two groups will constitute the local, year-round lunch and dinner segments. Secondary local markets include both corporate and government offices workers who will use the facilities for business lunches, business after hours, business meetings and special events such as Christmas parties, retirement functions, and so on. Their other secondary markets include the summer tourist and holiday shopper segments. They also determined that their facilities would not be conducive to weddings or bridal showers.

Services will include seven-day lunch service, six-day dinner service (no Sunday dinner), happy hour (Monday through Friday), and special events (Monday through Thursday theme nights and group functions in the upstairs facility). They determined that their target markets would not include breakfast, delivery service or Sunday dinner.

The Witches Brew will offer a widely varied menu of "fun foods" such as international and local appetizers, seasonal brews and related food specials, and a raw seafood bar, with moderate pricing (lunches $4-$8, dinners $5-$14). Their home brews will sell for $3-$5, a major money- maker with a mark-up of 1000+%).

Most of the towns within their working circle are growing at an annual rate of 5-10% in population. Real estate is appreciating at 10% per year. Because of the low crime rate, easy traffic flow, low tax rate, close proximity to Boston and other smaller regional cities, and trends in industry growth and jobs, the area exhibits all the signs of being very good for business for many years to come. With all the information collected and analysis completed, they drew up the sales forecast.

Sales Forecast*

Their best (educated) guess estimates follow:

	Units		Sales
80 lunches/day @$11 @340 days/year:	27,200	$	299,200
120 dinners/day @$17 @290 days/year	34,800		591,600
8 events/month corporate/gov't. @ $600	96		57,600
3 events/week theme nights @ $800	156		124,800
5 events/week happy hours @ $1100/day	260		286,000

Year One Sales Projection:	**$ 1,359,200**
	========
Year Two Sales Projection:	**$ 1,495,120**
	========
Year Three Sales Projection:	**$ 1,644,632**
	========

* Average revenue estimates per meal and per event include both food and beverage selections. The principles assumed a 10% per year increase in sales. While the principles have full confidence in these projections as a result of their intensive research and supporting documentation, their veteran advisors have strongly recommended they cut them back by 25% in their bank financing proposal.

Promotional Mix

The industry rule-of-thumb for spending on advertising, promotion and public relations is to keep expenditures to 3% of sales. The principles therefore included promotional mix budgets for $40,776, $44,854, and $49,339 (for years 1, 2, and 3).

On the basis of their market research and all the advice they've received, they prepared a mix of ads and promos that appeared in local papers, on selected radio and local cable spots, through chamber of commerce literature and releases, and on some roadway signs. They chose to retain and use the services of their local market research firm for advice on these ads and promos.

They also selected a package of school, sports, and community service causes and events to sponsor and participate in with a focus on building an image of a caring, responsible member of the local community. These included internship opportunities for local high school and college kids, the sponsoring of both a little league and adult baseball team, and an annual AIDS walk-a-thon.

Sales associates constitute another element of the promotional mix, but the principles decided to hold off on hiring any salespeople for now. They themselves will focus on the local year-round clientele. Tourists and Christmas shoppers will naturally flow to them given their good location, but the locals are the ones who will pay the bills and ultimately determine The Witches Brew's long-term success.

WEEKS 3 - 5 Student Activity

The Business Plan Connection

You may find this to be the most important and the most fun activity of the entire project. Your job now is simply to get out there and learn as much as you can about your competitors and your customers. The Business Description from your Week 1 Activity will again serve as your point of reference.

Rarely, if ever, is a proposed business venture a truly original idea. It is quite likely that there are already people out there doing what you are proposing to do. But don't let that discourage you. In fact, it may be an advantage. It gives you the opportunity to **ask questions**, **record observations**, and **gain many insights** into what it takes to establish and grow a successful business.

There are three things to do before you go out and ask people what's up in their business:

1. Create a list of places to go; just use the phone book.

2. Create a list of five or six questions to ask managers, owners or employees.

3. Create a list of things that you will need to observe and note.

Be sure to **select a wide range** of places to see. Consider large businesses, small businesses, national chains, private stores, city locations, and rural locations. Include the less obvious competitors along with the direct. For example, if you are proposing to start a sporting goods store, you would want to look into department stores and other places that sell sporting goods-- such as fitness clubs, golf courses, and so on-- in addition to sporting goods stores.

Your questions should be prioritized and focused. Ask the most important questions first in case you don't have a chance to ask all the questions you'd like. And **be consistent**. Asking the same questions will allow you to tabulate and analyze the responses more easily. Some examples include:

- What are your greatest strengths and most successful products and services?
- What is your biggest problem or challenge?
- Where do you see this industry going in the next five years?
- If you had it to do all over again, what would you do differently?
- What advice do you have for someone just starting out?

Make some observations. Take notes on:

- Location, traffic flow, parking, and neighboring stores.
- The storefront's appearance.
- The layout of the store or facility; check out displays, shelves, aisles, location of cash registers, music, lighting, and so on.
- Employee age, dress, selling technique, and attitude.

So how will you get people to speak with you? It's easy! Try these lines:

- Hello, I am a business student at _____, and I need your help and advice. When is the best time to ask you just a few questions?

- Hello, I am a business student at_____, and I plan to have your job someday! Would you please tell how you reached this position?

Note the tone of these approaches. One question asks for help and advice, while the other asks for someone's life story. Most people will respond favorably, but don't expect everyone to speak with you. Do not be discouraged if you hit an obstacle. You should expect about 7 out of 10 to cooperate. If you do not get this result, try a different approach.

You may feel a bit awkward or nervous at first. If possible, start with someone you know (current boss, former boss, friend's parent, neighbor). And once you get by the first interview or two, you'll be a pro; it's easy and fun. People love college students. Many students receive job offers as a result of this activity. After all, you are someone showing an interest in the business, you're smart and ambitious. Isn't that the type of person everyone wants to hire?

A question often asked is, "How many businesses should I visit and observe?" The answer is that you will know when you have asked enough. When you find yourself seeing and hearing the same thing over and over, it's time to stop asking questions and begin your data analysis. Results will vary by industry, and you'll need to keep your instructor's guidelines and course's time constraints in mind.

*   *   *

As for your customer base analysis, **rule out no one at first**. Draw that circle on a map with your business at the center.

Start with the **local town halls or city halls** (just as you did with the approval process). This time, however, you are after demographics and statistics about the population that are important to your business. This information may cover: population, age groups, growth trends, building permits, tax rates, schools, and so on.

The **county registry of deeds** may be the next stop. Here you will find an abundance of public information, similar to and extending beyond the data that you collected from town hall. Area chambers of commerce, government web sites, libraries, university research departments, and industry associations are other easy and usually free sources of useful information.

If time permits, and at the direction of your instructor, customer surveys can be developed, conducted, tabulated and analyzed. This will at least give you a taste of people's opinions, wants, needs, and preferences.

There is more "stuff" out there then you have time to read, so you need to focus your efforts. Take a few minutes to brainstorm your plans with friends or classmates. The questions of the day are: What information would I like to have about my prospective buying public, and, where and how can I most easily obtain that information?

*   *   *

There is a logical progression and a very specific outcome to this activity:

1. Competition Analysis:

   - Select and compile the best ideas, observations, and insights that you discover.
   - Avoid the inefficient, costly, and negative things that you've seen.
   - Create the "perfect business" given your goals and resources.

2. Customer Base Analysis:

   - Select the best specific target market groups within your working circle.
   - Study those groups closely.
   - Establish your promotional mix strategies and applications.

3. End Result:

   - Create your Sales Forecast (in both units of volume and dollars of sales) for the first one- to three-years of operation.

Tips for Success

1. Start with people you know.

2. Use the advice/help/compliment approach.

3. Show up on time, nicely dressed, and well prepared.

4. Just go out as a "shopper" and take notes.

5. Seek out the help of friendly, long-term town/city employees.

6. Consider a geographic location far away from your intended business. You are no longer a prospective competitor and may get better results and responses from business owners.

7. Have fun.

BPPRO SIDEBAR

Open BPPro and find your plan. Use the Task Wizard or the Plan Outline to find the "Keys to Success" topic. Read the explanation. Develop a short list of keys to success for the type of business you envision and write the Keys to Success topic into your plan.

Next find the chapter in the Market Analysis area that covers the type of business. Depending on whether or not you've used a sample plan, and whether your plan is set for detail or not (hint: this is in the Plan Setup phase of the Task Wizard), you'll find one or more standard topics with instructions and examples about the type of business you're in. Find those topics and fill them in for your business (hint: in a standard plan this starts with section 4.3, with the title "Industry Analysis" or "Service Business Analysis" or something similar).

CHAPTER 4

Case Study: The College Corner Store:

Do the financial projections support the proposed venture?

A note to the reader: This chapter case study and student activity focus on the accounting and financial components of a business plan. A glossary of all related accounting terminology is included in the student activity section. Regardless of your current knowledge and experience with accounting, rest assured that this is not a difficult component to work through. The math is basic arithmetic. The case study and student activity presentations are brief and to the point and remember that it in the real world it really just boils down to the "bottom line"-- Will we bring in more money than we spend?

Introduction

The College Corner Store is located on the main street in the heart of a small North Carolina college campus. Its main product lines include: soft drinks, beer, tobacco, cosmetics, snacks, newspapers, supplies, and some hot and cold food. You might say that it is a typical convenience store located in a typical college town.

The business has been around for more than thirty years, owned and operated by Johnny Gilmore, a fixture in the town and a friend to many students and locals. The building also includes three upstairs rental units. While Johnny has made a living over the years, the store is old and run-down. Tax returns for the past five years reveal stagnant sales and low profits. The business and the building are currently up for sale, as Johnny wants to retire. The asking price is $760,000.

A young couple, both local natives and graduates of the college, are actively pursuing the offer. They have signed a purchase and sale agreement pending financing and a satisfactory building inspection. Johnny likes the couple and wants to work with them, as he is interested in both their success and the continuation of his lifetime business. He has also indicated a willingness to assume part of the mortgage.

The young couple have completed an extensive market analysis. There are two direct competitors on campus, along with a few similar establishments in the local area. Johnny clearly has the best location of them all, for both the college and the local markets. The partners plan to renovate the retail business storefront and floor space and to try out several new ideas for products and services that will enhance both sales and profits. They have learned from their competition and customer base analysis that there are many ways to improve the performance of the business. Their longer-term plans call for a fourth rental/studio unit in the now vacant attic space.

One of the local banks is considering working with the partners and is interested in studying the Financial Plan section of their formal Business Plan. The bank has specifically requested the following:

- Sources and Uses Statement
- Projected Income (Profit & Loss) Statement
- Projected Cash Flow Statement
- Start-up Balance Sheet

The partners have considered the actual results of the past five years of operations (from Johnny's tax records), along with their market analysis findings, and have established a first-year sales projection of $632,000. They are ready to proceed with their Financial Plan report.

Relevant Issues and Actual Case Results

The sources and uses statement is considered the "cover page" to a financial proposal by many creditors and investors. It presents an itemized listing of the various sources of funding for a given project, along with the ways in which those dollars will be used.

The particulars for this case follow:

Sources and Uses Statement

Sources		Uses	
1. Partners Funds	$210,000	5. Building	$550,000
2. Bank Loan (LTD)	440,000	6. Renovations	80,000
3. Private Investor	210,000	7. Goodwill	210,000
4. Bank Loan (STD)	60,000	8. Working Capital	80,000
	$920,000		$920,000

Item 1:	The partners have $210,000 of their own funds for down payment ($110,000), renovations ($80,000), and cash reserves ($20,000).
Item 2:	The bank will provide a fifteen-year (long-term debt/LTD) note for 80% of the assessed value of the real estate ($550,000 @ 80% = $440,000).
Item 3:	This represents the second mortgage to be held by Johnny Gilmore.
Item 4:	The bank will provide a line-of-credit (short-term debt/STD) of $60,000.
Item 5:	The building and property was professionally assessed at $550,000.
Item 6:	The store will be shut down for one month and renovated.
Item 7:	This represents Johnny's desired return for the business name and goodwill established over the years.
Item 8:	This represents the buyer's cash reserves ($20,000) and available line-of-credit ($60,000).

Projected Income (Profit & Loss) Statement – Year 1

1. Sales		$ 632,000	
2. Cost of Goods Sold		300,000	
Gross Margin		$ 332,000	
3. Operating Expenses:		$ 254,000 (Sum of listed expenses)	
Payroll	$ 130,000		
Benefits	26,000		
Mortgages	56,000		
Depreciation	20,000		
Utilities	12,000		
Supplies	4,000		
Insurance	6,000		
Taxable Income		$ 78,000	
Taxes		23,400	
Net Income		$ 54,600	

Item 1:   Sales projection is based on past results of both store and rental units, plus 15%, which the partners consider to be conservative given the changes they plan.

Item 2:   Partners have used the industry standard of 100% mark-up ($300,000 of merchandise selling for $600,000); the extra $32,000 of sales revenues is rental income.

Item 3:   Operating expenses are based on past amounts for both store and rental units, plus new mortgages and related depreciation.

Projected Cash Flow Statement – Year 1
(in 000's)

	June	July	Aug	Sept	Oct	Nov	Dec	Jan	Feb	Mar	Apr	May	Total Year
Cash In:	$0	$34	$45	$65	$63	$60	$50	$40	$65	$60	$70	$80	$632
Cash Out:	$46	$46	$46	$46	$46	$46	$46	$46	$46	$46	$46	$46	$554
Net Cash Flow:	($46)	($12)	($ 1)	$19	$17	$14	$ 4	($ 6)	$19	$14	$24	$34	$ 78
Beginning Balance:	$80	$34	$22	$21	$40	.....	.....	.....	.....	.....	.....	.....	
Ending Balance:	$34	$22	$21	$40	.....	.....	.....	.....	.....	.....	.....	.....	

Supporting notes:

- The store will be closed for renovations during June, thus no sales/no cash-in.
- Cash inflows from September forward are based on historical amounts adjusted for projected new sales.
- Cash outflows are based on past historical amounts adjusted for projected new expenses and new mortgages.
- The partners will exhaust their cash reserves during the first month and will begin to use their line-of-credit ($0 cash in minus $46 cash out).
- The business finally begins to "carry itself" during September ($65 cash in minus $46 cash out).
- The partners will be able to pay down their line-of-credit during September, October, and November.

Start-up Balance Sheet – June 1, 20--

Current Assets		Current Liabilities	
Cash	$ 17,000	Accounts Payables	$ 35,000
Inventory	35,000	Notes Payable	0
Accounts Receivables	0	(line-of-credit)	
Pre-paid Expenses	3,000		
Fixed Assets		**Long-Term Liabilities**	
Land	$ 20,000		$440,000
Building	550,000	**Stock/Owner's Equity**	
Equipment	60,000	Stock	$210,000
	$685,000		**$685,000**
	======		======

Supporting notes:

- The partners have $17,000 of remaining cash reserves (their original $210,000 less $110,000 down payment at closing, less $80,000 for renovations, less $3,000 for pre-paid expenses = $17,000).
- Partners were able to stock the store with merchandise/inventory through their vendors credit (accounts payables $35,000)
- As of the June 1st, the line-of-credit has not yet been used (notes payable $0).
- The "Stock" of $210,000 represents Johnny's second mortgage.

End Notes

The bank loan officer had a few questions regarding some of the partners' figures. But the market research documentation along with the seller's past financial statements and tax returns satisfied the bank, and the loan was approved.

The partners were very wise to negotiate a second mortgage with Johnny. The second mortgage filled the gap with the funding necessary to allow the transaction to take place ($210,000). The partners will pay off that loan with revenues generated from business operations rather than from their own money or the bank's. Along with that second mortgage with Johnny, the partners have his interest and invaluable experience to help them through their start-up period.

The partners also plan to use revenues generated from business operations to renovate the attic and establish a fourth rental unit by year two.

Some banks may require an extension of the financial projections through year two or three of operations. This was not required in this case, although the partners did project an annual 10% growth in sales. Some banks may also require a more detailed breakdown of certain line items.

WEEKS 6 - 7 Student Activity

The Business Plan Connection

With your sales forecast in hand (the dollars-and-cents conclusion drawn from your market research), it is now time to turn your attention to the financial side of the proposed business venture. In particular, you must address the following questions and issues:

- How much funding will you need to start the business?
- Will your proposed business venture make money?
- How much funding will you need to carry the business until it can carry itself?
- Do the overall financial projections meet your goals?

There is a logical sequence to building the financial plan section of your Business Plan. Let's keep it simple and quick. Do not allow yourself to get bogged down over a single line item. Your goal initially is to create a rough first draft which can then be expanded, edited, and revised as necessary.

Step 1: Create your first-year income (profit &loss) statement: Begin with sales revenues (your sales forecast) which is always the first line of any income statement.

The question now becomes **What will it take in terms of expenses to generate those sales revenues?** We now "work from the top down" to create the statement. The standard format looks like this:

Sales	$
-Cost of Sales	_____
=Gross Margin	$
(or Gross Profit)	
-Operating Expenses	$
Payroll	
Mortgage/Rent	
Utilities	
Insurance	
Supplies	
Advertising	
Etc.; list each	_____
=Taxable Income	$
-Taxes (assume 30%)	_____
=Net Income	$
	=====

Now just fill in the blanks to the best of your ability. As you move down from line to line, keep asking yourself that question-- What will it take to generate those sales revenues (how much merchandise, how many employees, how much insurance, and so on). In addition to the information that you have collected, rely on your own common sense and work experience to estimate line items.

Be as realistic as possible. You will find that the list of expenses is easy to create. The information is readily available and quite predictable. The sales number is the most difficult to establish and determine. Remember that this sales forecast is never anything more than an educated guess. The tendency is to overestimate sales, especially for the first year. A good rule-of-thumb is to reduce your first year sales estimate by 25%.

Step 2: Create your first year cash flow statement: The question now becomes: **When will the sales revenues physically come in to the business, and when will the expenses actually be paid?** Again, we now work from the top down to create the statement. The standard format follows:

Cash In	$
-Cash Out	$
	_____
=Net Cash Flow	$
+Beginning Balance	
	_____
=Ending Balance	$
	=====

The difference between "sales" and "cash in" for the period is the change in accounts receivables (if any). In other words, have you collected all of the reported sales, or do customers still owe you money? For example, if sales for a given year are $500,000 and the accounts receivables account is $100,000 more than it was at the beginning of that year, it means that only $400,000 was actually received by the business ("cash-in").

The difference between "operating expenses" and "cash out" is determined in the same manner. In other words, have you paid all of the reported expenses, or do you still owe money to various suppliers? For example, if the cost of sales for a given year are $250,000 and the accounts payables account is $50,000 more than it was at the beginning of the year, it means that only $200,000 was actually paid to suppliers ("cash-out").

The cash flow statement is especially important to the bank. It has become one of their most important measures of your ability to get and to repay the loan the bank has given you.

Again, just fill in the blanks to the best of your ability. If you plan to operate a cash business, your sales and cash in figures will be the same. If you plan to operate a business where credit must be extended, then your cash in figures will also include sales from prior periods or months. In other words, cash in will lag behind sales (a portion of sales generated in June will be collected in July and August and so on). The same holds true for using credit and the timing of corresponding cash outs. Merchandise/inventory purchased and sold during one month may be paid for in subsequent months.

When it comes to a cash flow statement for a new business, being as realistic as possible means expecting a slow start in sales revenues. It is not unusual for a new business to take six-months to eighteen-months to finally begin to carry itself. It takes time for the word to get out. It takes time to build a steady clientele and a steady flow of cash.

Having adequate working capital means having enough cash (your own) and/or access to cash (the line-of-credit) at the start of your operations to carry you through to the time when your business will support itself. This money must also cover your necessary personal living expenses. You must continue to pay your rent and other bills.

The bank will view you in a much more favorable light and you will have greater credibility if you have a realistic outlook towards cash flow. Always try to establish a line-of-credit that is more than you think you will need. You pay interest only on what you actually use or borrow. Try to avoid running out of cash. You'll look bad, and your business may fail.

Step 3: Create your start-up balance sheet: The balance sheet captures your financial position at a moment in time. It looks at your assets, liabilities, and owner's equity position. The standard format looks like this:

Current Assets:		Current Liabilities:	
Cash	$	Accounts Payable	$
Accounts Receivable		Notes Payable	
Inventory		(line-of-credit)	
Pre-paid Expenses			
Fixed Assets:		Long-term Liabilities:	
Land	$	Long-term Debt	$
Buildings			
Equipment		Owner's Equity:	
Vehicles			
		Stock/Investors	$
		Owner's Net Worth	
	$	=	$
	=====		=====

31

Note that the bottom-half of this statement represents the start-up of your business. The land, buildings, equipment and vehicles required to build the business are funded by some combination of your money, the bank's money, and your investors' money.

The top-half represents the day-to-day operations of your business. You purchase inventory (through cash, accounts payable or notes payable) and sell it to customers (receiving cash or increasing accounts receivable) at a higher rate. This excess of cash-in over cash-out "spills out" of the balance sheet to cover other expenses (from the income statement) and if sales are strong enough-- to generate profits.

Step 4: Create your Sources and Uses statement: This statement may serve as the cover or summary page to the financial plan section of your Business Plan. The standard format looks like this:

Sources		Uses	
Your Money	$	Land, Buildings,	$
The Bank's Money	$	Equipment, Vehicles	
Private Investors	$	Renovations	$
Other Sources	$	Goodwill	$
		Working Capital	$
	$	=	$
	=====		=====

This document summarizes the total cost of your start-up project.

Here are some pointers you may find useful. Banks are conservative and limit their lending. You will often need to have at least 25% of the total cost of the project available through your own funds and/or sources other than the bank. Banks need to see measurable fixed assets before making a loan. Adequate working capital (access to cash) must be available to pay the bills until the business begins to support itself.

Tips for Success

- Go to at least one bank or lending institution and get a copy of a loan application to find out what that bank or institution requires before making a loan.

- Go to at least one other possible source of funding, which could be family members, a private investor, a government program (the Small Business Administration or the Department of Commerce for example), an insurance company, a business owner or some other person or institution you might think of. There are many sources and many lending requirements. It may be worth your while to investigate.

- Keep it simple. Follow the statement formats presented in this book and in the **Business Plan Pro** software. Just fill in the blanks one by one.

- Be realistic, especially on the sales side of your forecasting.

- Last, but not least, learn as much as you can about this country's financial system and the many ways funds flow and change hands. Learn the system so that you can benefit. Learn to make the system work for you.

CHAPTER 4

<u>Glossary of Accounting Terminology</u>

Accounts Payable: The dollar amount shown (on the current liability portion of the balance sheet) represents money currently owed to suppliers for merchandise/inventory purchases.

Assets: Assets are anything of value that the business owns and has possession of, such as cash, inventory, accounts receivables, pre-paid expenses, land, buildings, equipment and vehicles.

Balance Sheet: The balance sheet is a summary statement of all assets, liabilities and stock/owner's equity for a business on a given date.

Benefits (Payroll): The dollar amount shown (on the expense portion of the income statement) is the sum of all employee-related expenses beyond wages, such as health insurance, uniforms, unemployment and social security, and so on.

Business Name (Goodwill): This is a negotiated dollar amount between the buyer and seller of a business above and beyond the value of all tangible assets. It represents the intangible value of the reputation, industry name and image in the community that a business owner has established during his or her tenure. There is no accounting formula to determine this. Its aim is to measure the value of future sales and profits that a new owner might expect to "inherit".

Cash Flow Statement: The cash flow statement indicates the specific date and/or time period during which a business actually receives and spends money.

Depreciation: The dollar amount shown (on the expense portion of the income statement) is the sum of the "calculated loss in value" of all fixed assets of a business (buildings, equipment and vehicles) over time. It is based on the original cost of each asset, and on a pre-determined schedule based on the expected years of service of each fixed asset. There are several schedule options for the business owner to choose from.

Income (Profit and Loss) Statement: An income statement reports all sales revenues, expenses and profits for a business for a given period of time regardless of whether the business has actually received or spent those funds.

Insurance: The dollar amount shown (on the expense portion of the income statement) is the sum of all forms of insurance that the business carries beyond those listed under benefits, such as liability, fire, inventory, flood, and so on.

Inventory (and the connection to **Cost of Goods Sold/Cost of Sales**): The dollar amount shown (on the current asset portion of the balance sheet) is the sum total of all raw materials and/or merchandise purchased by a business for manufacturing and selling purposes. When merchandise/inventory is sold, that dollar amount is removed from the inventory account and added to the cost of goods sold/cost of sales line item on the income statement.

Liabilities: The dollar amounts shown (on both the current and long-term liability portions of the balance sheet) represent debt/money owed by the business to its suppliers, bankers and other creditors.

Long-term Debt: The dollar amount shown (on the long-term liability portion of the balance sheet) represents the current balance of all loans. Long-term debt typically represents periods of five or more years for the purchase of land, buildings, equipment and vehicles.

Notes Payable (and the connection to the **Line-of-Credit**): The dollar amount shown (on the current liability portion of the balance sheet) is the sum of all money owed to the bank. This is typically a short-term loan used exclusively for the purchase of merchandise/inventory.

Parenthesis ( ): This is an accounting symbol used to indicate a negative number.

Pre-paid Expenses: The dollar amount shown (on the current assets portion of the balance sheet) represents a dollar amount already spent for something not yet used. This typically represents the purchase of business insurance.

Stock (and the connection to **Second Mortgages/Private Investors/Venture Capitalists**): The dollar amount shown (on the owner's equity/net worth portion of the balance sheet) represents the dollar amount invested/owned by private individuals and other non-bank entities who may invest and own a percentage of a business.

Supplies: The dollar amount shown (on the expense portion of the income statement) represents materials needed to operate the business not including merchandise/inventory, such as paper wrapping, bags, small tools, office supplies, bathroom supplies and so on.

Utilities: The dollar amount shown (on the expense portion of the income statement) represents the total cost of electricity, oil, gas, and other forms of energy required to operate a business for a given time period.

Working Capital (and the connection to **cash** and the **line-of-credit**): This represents the cash on hand at any given time and/or the cash needed to sustain business operations. Cash is available from the owner's personal funds, from sales revenues generated by the business and from the bank line-of-credit (short-term borrowing).

CHAPTER 5

Case Study: Pacific Coast Forest Products;

A Company in Need of Organization and Structure

Introduction

Pacific Coast Forest Products is a manufacturing facility spread over forty acres on two locations near the Oregon coast. The company also manages 60,000 acres of privately owned forestland. The staff, equipment, and facilities convert trees into logs, lumber, and a variety of wood products that are sold all over the world through both wholesale distribution channels (middlemen) and direct sales (retail, consumers, other end-users). Facilities include three sawmills that convert logs to lumber, six dry kilns where the wood is dried, a planer mill that converts rough-cut lumber to very specific dimensions and surface patterns and a processing plant that converts lumber into cut-to-size products and furniture parts.

The company was established during World War II. It provided ammunition boxes, planking for ships and docks, and building materials for the U.S. military. After the war, the processing plant converted its product lines to fruit and fish boxes, and the sawmills continued to produce lumber for a variety of domestic markets.

During the early 1980's, a large conglomerate purchased the business. The new owners came onto the scene with money to spend and a great vision for a more productive and diversified future. The investment was attractive because the price was right, access to raw materials and markets was good, and there was room to grow in terms of production, efficiency, and new market capabilities.

On the personnel side, the new owners inherited a situation with many challenges. The company employed 125 people directly, along with an additional 40 sub-contractors working in the woods. Morale was extremely low and turnover was extremely high. There were almost no managers, no office or sales department, no documented rules or guidelines, and unsafe and unattractive working conditions. The former owner also left behind a marginal reputation within the industry and the community. The new owners immediately gave the business a new name-- Pacific Coast Forest Products.

The board of directors hired three corporate officers to run the company. The president and vice president of finance and administration were brought in from the outside; the vice president of personnel was hired from within.

The board of directors set three very specific goals for the first three years of operation:

- Increase production by 30%.
- Shift the current wholesale sales - direct sales mix from 80%-20% to 50%-50%.
- Increase net profit performance from the current 4% to 10% (net income to sales).

Actual Results

The top managers recognized that the secret to achieving the corporate goals was almost exclusively a personnel issue. The facilities, raw materials, and markets were all there for the taking, but there was absolutely no way of reaching their production, sales and profit goals under the current mode of operation.

They began with a series of meetings with the total staff and with the individual departments. The meetings were aimed at communicating the new company's goals in a positive way and at soliciting input and ideas from as many people as possible. After all, the people performing each job know as much or more about their job than anyone else.

The new top managers were wise to address the high turnover and low morale issues head-on through positive communications and through employee participation in the decision-making process. They made it very clear that things would be different from now on and that everyone who was willing to become a part of the team would keep their job and have a bright future.

After three months of meetings, observing operations, studying the market, and analyzing a variety of data (including all of the employee's input and ideas), the top managers prepared a formal organizational chart and presented it to the employees for review, revision, and implementation. The top managers were also sure to incorporate the production and sales goals into their overall personnel needs assessment. The final draft, which carries the overwhelming consensus and support of all employees follows:

ORGANIZATIONAL CHART

Pacific Coast Forest Products

President

VP Sales & Marketing   **VP Finance/Administration**   **VP Production & Personnel**

Sales Manager   **Office Manager**   **Mill 1 Manager**   **Mill 2 Manager**   **Mill 3 Manager**

Inside Sales-2   Accounting-2   Production   Production   Production
Outside Sales-1   Office Staff-4   Staff-14   Staff-8   Staff-8
Support Staff-1

Planer Mill Manager   **Products Division Manager**   **Maintenance & Safety Manager**

Production   Production   Production
Staff-14   Staff-20   Staff-14

Woodlands Manager   **Transportation Manager**

Foresters-4   Shipping-8

An organizational chart is useful in many ways. It presents a picture of each of the parts that make up the whole. It gives workers an opportunity to appreciate the role they play in the overall mission of the company. It presents a picture of a well-thought-out program. It also opens itself to improvement through change.

Note that the total number of employees has been reduced from the original 125 to 114 (14 managers and 100 production staff). But thanks to the combination of changing some production procedures and creating a more cohesive and more motivated team, this smaller group readily accepted the challenge of producing 30% more product than in the past.

With a good picture in hand-- the organizational chart-- it was now time to establish a written job description for each position. The managers realized that this would be most successful as a two-way process, that is, each employee participates in the creation of their job description. Employees are always more motivated to perform under such cooperative circumstances.

A complete and meaningful job description has three main components.

Job Responsibilities: What are the position's specific tasks and how long does each task take? Most companies do a good job with this component; unfortunately, it is often the only component they write up.

Job Authority: What decision-making power goes with the position? It is important to let people do their job, to delegate responsibility, and to include some flexibility and room for judgment. Motivation and performance will be enhanced under such trusting circumstances. Many job descriptions do not include this component.

Job Accountability: How will management measure an individual's performance? This measurement must be objective, not subjective. Results such as new accounts, production quotas, downtime, and attendance can and should be agreed on by manager and employee and measured. Results such as attitude, responsibility, and vision are subjective and much more difficult to measure.

In theory, if every individual within an organization meets or exceeds the expectations of their job descriptions, the company will achieve or exceed its goals. In practice, managers realize that perfection is impossible and generally would settle with coming within 5% of their goals.

The top managers worked with the board of directors to establish their own job descriptions. The top managers in turn worked with department managers and the process was completed as each department manager worked with each of his or her own staff.

One year later at the company picnic, the president delivered a short speech: "It has been so gratifying to see us all come together and work as a team. We were able to work out the production bugs, effect other changes, and come within 4% of our established goals. We are well on our way to long-term success, and we are pleased to be able to share the wealth with our employees through our current and future incentive programs".

WEEK 8 Student Activity

The Business Plan Connection

At this point, you should have conducted extensive market research that resulted in the creation of a sales forecast. That sales forecast allowed you to create a set of projected financial statements.

Now you will once again use your sales forecast, along with your income (profit and loss) statement. The focus shifts from money to people. Take a few moments to study your income statement and to envision your business in operation. The question to address is: **How many people will it take to turn your income statement into reality?**

Start at the top of your income statement and **create an organizational chart** similar to the one presented in Case 3, Pacific Coast Forest Products. Imagine the number of marketing and sales people it will take to achieve your projected level of sales. Do the same with all of your other departments (for example, production, shipping and receiving, and maintenance).

Next consider your management team. How much supervision will it take to oversee the total operation? The answer will vary greatly depending on many variables such as the skills and education of your employees, customer expectations, hours of operation, number of locations, and so on. How many managers are "just right"? Take the time to edit and revise your organizational chart until it looks perfect to you.

The focus now shifts to job descriptions. **Establish a job description for each individual, from your president to your custodian**. Again, refer to the Case 3 model and/or to your instructor for guidance in this matter. For the sake of time, your instructor may have you consolidate job descriptions by work function or group. Be sure to include each of the three main components (responsibilities, authority, and accountability) in each job description.

Your final activity is to take a step back and envision the results of your organizational chart and collection of job descriptions in action. Will the plans you've drawn up get the job done? Do you have too many people, too few, or just the right number? Ask yourself the same question with regard to your managers. Have you provided enough detail for each component of each job description? Could you walk into any job that you have described and fully understand what to do, what decision-making power you have, and how you will be evaluated? Once it all makes sense, you have completed this portion of your Business Plan.

BPPRO SIDEBAR

Open your BPPro business plan and find the section titled "Management Team". If you haven't already, fill in the topics included in Management Team including the Personnel Plan table. Then compare your sales per employee in the Business Ratios table to the industry average sales per employee. How does your business compare to the industry averages? Can you explain the differences?

Use your sample plan browser to open each of the three sample plans you chose for the sidebar exercise in Chapter 2. Read the management team chapters of each of those plans. How are they different? Are the differences related to the different types of business, or to other factors such as the size of the business, the numbers of years in business or something else? How do these plans compare to their respective industry standards for sales per employee?

CHAPTER 6

Case Study: Spectacular Video & Entertainment Center;

Location, Layout, and Operations Management

Introduction

Nathan and Tim Mc Daniel, brothers and business partners, have completed a successful market and financial analysis of their proposed venture. Spectacular Video & Entertainment Center will specialize in video and equipment rentals and sales and a mix of complementary products that include snacks, gift certificates, software and parts, installation and service.

At this time, all permits, approvals and licenses are in place, their current and long-term market outlook and position are excellent, and their financing package is set. In addition, the area has an abundance of qualified employees at all levels.

Nathan and Tim's focus, and the focus of this case and its related student activity is on selecting the best location option, setting up the layout of both the storefront and inside floor space of the site and establishing day-to-day operating procedures.

Nathan and Tim have trimmed their location option list to three possible spots.

The first is a stand-alone building located at a busy intersection. Traffic flow, visibility and parking are excellent. The building is currently home to one of a chain of drug stores that will discontinue operations at that location. The building, available for lease or for a lease/buy option is located in the larger of two neighboring towns under consideration, and has two direct, nearby competitors. It is the largest and most expensive of the three locations.

The second store is available for rent. It is part of a four-store mini-mall and four-unit apartment building in the neighboring smaller town. It has the lowest volume of traffic flow of the three locations, and has good visibility and parking. It is the least expensive of the three.

The third choice is a store located in a new, twelve-store strip mall adjacent to a busy traffic rotary, also in the smaller neighboring town. The mall features a large, super market chain store, a moderately-sized drug store chain-store, and ten smaller stores of varying size. Traffic flow, visibility and parking are excellent. The store is available for a lease ranging from two, to ten years, with an option to renew. It is moderately priced--slightly below that of the stand-alone building.

Relevant Issues and Questions

There is an old saying that goes, **When selecting real estate, there are only three things that matter: location, location, and location.**

And sometimes location is crucial to success. For restaurants, hotels, and retail stores, it is often a major criterion. In other instances, location matters less. For businesses such as an accounting firm, a building contractor or a consultant, location may be unimportant. Nathan and Tim concluded that the location of their business is a high priority.

When analyzing location, consider these major factors.

- Traffic count and flow: How much traffic goes by each day, and how visible and accessible is the building to passers-by?
- Parking: Is there enough? This is a BIG problem for many businesses.
- Neighboring stores: Who are they? Will they draw customers to your store?
- The neighborhood: How safe is it, especially at night?
- Future traffic flow plans: What lies ahead for road expansion or other projects that might result in changes to traffic flow patterns or even permanent detours?
- Future area growth: What lies ahead for population and economic growth for the area?
- Cost and availability: How much will your location cost? Consider renting, leasing and buying options. Buying the building is often the preferred choice. Buying would provide long-term security, more predictable fixed costs and the opportunity to benefit from your own real estate value appreciation over time.

When analyzing layout, keep these major questions in mind.

- How visible is the business from the road? How appealing is the storefront to passersby? What are the best strategies for signs, lights, and other attention getters?
- What is the best use of your inside space? What is the best way to maximize sales and profits per square foot of floor space?
- What is the best physical layout for customers? What is the best way to "herd" customers through the store and to minimize customer shoplifting? What is the best way to maximize product exposure, impulse buying, and total purchases?
- What is the best layout for employees? What is most efficient in terms of employee comfort and productivity?
- What other concerns might there be? They may include inventory management and storage areas, places for employee work breaks and restrooms for employees and customers. Management may also consider safety and security issues, the best use of wall and ceiling space, and so on.

When analyzing day-to-day operations and procedures, think about these points.

- The most logical and profitable hours of operation.
- Procedures for opening and closing the business each day.
- Procedures for nightly deposits.
- Policies for on-site vendors and suppliers.
- A daily and weekly maintenance and clean-up schedule.
- Safety and first-aid procedures.
- Customer service policies and practices.

Actual Results of Case

After many hours of brainstorming, data analysis, and discussions with advisors, Nathan and Tim selected the twelve-store strip mall adjacent to the busy traffic rotary as the location for their business. They saw these advantages in this location:

- The highest current and long-term profit potential
- The least amount of direct competition
- The high traffic and customer volume of neighboring stores
- The moderate cost
- The highly visible location with ample parking

They agreed to a five-year lease with renewal options and negotiated a written right of first refusal-- which means they get the first chance to buy it-- should the owners ever decide to sell.

The stand-alone location was rejected because of its high cost and more intense level of competition. Nathan and Tim also found that neighborhood to have the highest crime rate.

Though the least expensive of the three, the rental unit in the four-store mini-mall was rejected because of the past history of failed businesses in that location and because of the low traffic volume. The partners also considered the location to be the least convenient and customer-friendly.

The partners installed a large lighted sign to the outside of the building that was easily seen by passers-by from all directions, a colorful awning that protected customers from the weather and a handy after-hours video drop box that was accessible to both drive-by and foot traffic.

The store was nicely sandwiched between the super market and the drug store, by far the busiest of all of the mall stores. The overall appearance and presentation of the storefront was inviting, thanks to some consultation from a local marketing and public relations firm.

The partners carefully set up their floor displays and fixtures incorporating the best ideas and observations from their earlier competition analysis that included an industry-proven floor plan from one of the national video store chains. A security system was set up at the front door adjacent to the check-out/register area.

Retail products and impulse items were strategically placed at the check-out/register area and at key locations throughout the store. For example, drinks and snacks were located adjacent to the registers. New releases were located at the rear of the store requiring customers to pass by a variety of other products along the way. Shelf height and spacing used the latest in customer ergonomics. This has to do with the physical movements and comfort of customers, such as placing high profit items in easy to see and reach locations, providing comfortable aisle widths for travel, room temperature and lighting, and so on. All shelves and aisles were placed at forty-five degree angles to the walls so that customers could be herded to the corners of the room, which contributed to the fullest use of available floor and wall space. Products and promotional themes hung from the ceiling, and wall space was fully used.

The room was brightly decorated and pleasing to the eye. TV screens were strategically placed by product line to allow the partners to promote a mix of products and give customers the opportunity to sample products. Restrooms, kept immaculately clean, were available for both employees and customers.

As for day-to-day operations and procedures, a formal company handbook was distributed to employees during their orientation and training period. The handbook covered topics ranging from customer service, to opening and closing procedures, the maintenance schedule, and employee expectations. It was often revised as the partners gained experience, employees offered input at staff meetings, the partners continued in assessing the competition and the market, and customers provided feedback.

Nathan and Tim were very pleased with their accomplishments. They had taken the time to study the location, layout, and operations aspects of their business and industry and had been-- and remained-- open to suggestions from many parties. And they had taken the advice of an old professor who often reminded them to work hard to "do it right the first time" which resulted in the least amount of work and expense, and the highest amount of profits!

WEEKS 9 – 10 Student Activity

The Business Plan Connection

You should find this to be a fascinating and fun activity. You may already have a head start on this as a result of your competition analysis activities and research.

Now that you have a vision of your customer base and the projected level of sales that you plan to achieve, the focus now shifts to your physical plant and production process.

The physical plant is the building that you have selected to buy, lease, rent or build and its location. The production process is how the floor of the building is laid out and what your day-to-day procedures are. **What will it take in terms of facilities and employee procedures to accommodate your customers and achieve your desired levels of sales and profits?**

Regardless of which of the three major categories that your business falls into (retail, service, manufacturing), you should embrace the "production mentality". The production mentality focuses on generating the highest volume and quality of (sales) units at the lowest cost. This is a natural thing to do in a manufacturing situation. Raw materials are processed through a series of steps and machines, operated by employees, to produce the highest quality product for the least cost.

Retail and service businesses really do the same thing. A retail business "processes" customers through its doors. The retail establishment must be set up with the right features, fixtures, employees, and logistics for the business to get the most sales for the least cost. In a service business, the product is the service itself. Your employees must have procedures and the necessary vehicles and/or equipment to provide the highest quality service at the lowest cost. Whatever the type of business, the goal is to maximize customer sales and profits.

Your job at this time, is to just "get out there" and observe and take notes on three distinct topics: location, layout, and operations management procedures. The Spectacular Video & Entertainment Center case study (a retail and service business) provides the guidelines for this research and data collection. Your instructor will provide his or her specific requirements.

Those of you using the **Business Plan Pro** software addressed the issues of location and facilities as part of your **Section 2.0 Company Summary**. This chapter and student activity allow you to expand on these considerations and add much more detail, now that you have a more complete vision of your business. Also note the connection between the job descriptions that you prepared and your day-to-day operations procedures.

Some of you may have a business that you can run out of a home office (hair salon, accountant, consultant, artist, technician, sales associate, contractor, architect, and many others). This set-up may offer tax and lifestyle advantages. But it is still important to establish an efficient layout and set of procedures for operations, making sure you service customers well, control costs and maximize profits.

At the completion of this activity and section of your Business Plan, you should have selected a specific location, should have a description of the specific layout of that facility, and should have an operations/procedures manual/summary.

BPPRO SIDEBAR

The BPPro does not cover location, layout, and operations management to the extent and detail as does this chapter. We therefore recommend that you complete this student activity on a word document and include it as part of your BPPro section 2.0 Company Summary and/or as another component of your Plan Outline.

Open your BPPro plan and go to section 2.0 Company Summary. Make sure you fill in all of the topics and tables included in that section, particularly the start-up costs, or, if you are developing a plan for an already existing company, the past performance. Explain why you've chosen your particular form of business entity (proprietorship, partnership, corporation and so on).

Now use the sample plan browser to find two comparable sample business plans. Look for plans in similar industries, or similar types of business. Read through their company chapters to see what they have chosen as a form of ownership and why.

CHAPTER 7

Case Study: The Metropolitan Real Estate Cooperative;

Independent Brokers in Need of Administrative Support

General Introduction

Let's define administration as any and all "office-type" activities and functions necessary for the company to achieve its goals. **While administrative activities and functions vary from company to company, they commonly include tasks that fall outside of the well-defined areas of marketing and sales, finance, personnel and operations management (chapters 3 through 6).**

These administrative activities include, but are not limited to:

- Supporting general office functions (phone/fax/email, document prep/copy, mail)
- Setting up meetings
- Handling legal, insurance, and tax issues
- Managing payroll
- Seeing to public and community relations activities
- Processing orders
- Shipping/Receiving/Storing
- Offering tech support
- Managing facilities services (food, restrooms, janitorial)
- Handling environmental and safety issues
- Supervising transportation

Of course, your business may have other administrative functions. However you treat these tasks, all that matters is that the total job gets done

Some businesses and industries categorize all of the above bulleted items as "cost center" activities. Cost centers include functions that must take place in order for the company to achieve its goals. Cost centers usually do not generate revenues or profits, hence the name. The mission of these centers is to get the job done for the lowest cost.

Case Particulars and Results

This case focuses on the administrative side of a real estate business. It also introduces you to strategies for sharing the costs of common needs with competitors and to the use of outside vendors and sub-contractors.

Most real estate sales associates begin their careers with established agencies, which are often national franchises. This set-up occurs because state regulators require a new associate to be sponsored by an established agency and to work through an apprentice period following the successful completion of a real estate course and exam.

Starting off this way makes sense because most existing real estate agencies have an established clientele, a fully functioning office and support staff and a formal training program.

Following the apprentice period, some associates choose to become an independent licensed real estate broker. This step usually requires the successful completion of a second exam along with some work experience. This next level on the industry ladder comes with the right to sell real estate on your own, to establish your own agency, and to possibly make more money.

Some independent brokers from the New York-New Jersey metropolitan area have decided to form an administrative cooperative, meaning shared office space and shared administrative costs. These individuals are longtime colleagues who have moved up the ranks together over the years. They have all achieved financial success and career satisfaction as independent brokers but find themselves needing some of the administrative support services we mentioned earlier.

The group of nine brokers rented two offices, one in Northern New Jersey and one in Manhattan. The Metropolitan Real Estate Cooperative provides administrative support services to all nine brokers who share the cost.

Four secretaries answer nine separate phone lines, take and deliver messages, prepare documents, arrange meetings, and maintain a real estate library and nationwide computer network, along with other traditional office functions. One paralegal performs all deed research and prepares standard documents and packages for transaction closings. Both offices have a conference room.

. Additional customer services such as financing, insurance, moving and storage arrangements, temporary housing, transportation and title and legal services are provided to round out the "one-stop-shop" real estate service. Each of the nine brokers continues to work out of his or her home office, which provides some tax advantages.

The end result is that the total job gets done for each independent broker for the lowest cost. The brokers are free to focus their time and efforts on what they do best-- showing and selling real estate.

WEEK 11 Student Activity

The Business Plan Connection

As you now know, there are many details that must come together so that your business will function smoothly and profitably.

The goals of this chapter are: for you to tie-up any and all loose ends, to think ahead and avoid unwanted surprises, to answer any remaining questions, and to complete the contents of your Business Plan.

First create a list of any remaining details that you need to attend to, using a four-step process:

1. Read over your entire Business Plan to date and revisit your observations and interview notes.

2. Envision the physical plant-- your land, buildings, and equipment. What functions, activities, and services will it take to maintain those facilities that are not yet documented?

3. Now consider your day-to-day operations. Think about your employees, your customers, and your suppliers. Walk through a typical day from opening to closing. What else have you forgotten?

4. Think about the outside agencies that you must deal with-- local, state, and federal offices, banks, insurance companies, regulators, suppliers, customers, shippers, and so on. Have you covered all bases?

Now take this list of remaining details and try to find a home for each item in your already established job descriptions. Who can get the job done? Will you need more people or more positions than you previously thought? Will you need to contract vendors or subcontractors from the outside to fulfill some requirements?

Those of you who have used the **Business Plan Pro** software may find an appropriate place among the many subcategories within each **Section** of the **Table of Contents** for your missing details and job functions. Those of you have used the Exhibit 1 Guide for the Creation of a Business Plan from Chapter 1 should do the same. For example, the need for an additional sales associate can be incorporated into your organizational chart. The need for payroll administration tasks can be added to your bookkeeper's job description.

Congratulations! Your research and data collection are now complete. The final step, covered in the next chapter is preparing and presenting your Business Plan.

BPPRO SIDEBAR

At this point you are ready to complete the contents of your business plan. Open BPPro and use the Easy Plan Wizard that takes you through every step of the plan from start to finish. As you click your way from start to finish, add any remaining task or subject that applies to your plan and drop any that do not.

If you have found a home for each of the remaining details covered in this chapter your work is done. If not, you once again have the option to click the Plan Outline to access your table of contents and to add both a new section and word file to your existing plan.

CHAPTER 8

The Professional Presentation

Perspective

Our focus now shifts from content to presentation. At this point, you have compiled a tremendous volume and variety of information (Chapters 2 through 7), some of which will become the content of your Business Plan. In presenting this information, we consider the Plan's appearance, organization and flow, spelling, grammar, and ease of readability.

Remember that our job as business owners and managers is to set and achieve goals through putting well-thought-out decisions into action. Achieving goals almost always depends on the support and cooperation of many people, both inside and outside of the company. And the degree of support and cooperation that you receive will result from your ability to communicate, both orally and in writing. In this chapter we'll focus on your written communication as it appears in your Business Plan.

The goal of this chapter is creating your final draft Business Plan.

The Writing Process

The first step in the writing process is <u>audience analysis</u>. Who will read your Business Plan? What are their expectations? What is their level of understanding of the subject matter? What obstacles and challenges must you overcome? What questions must you answer? What are your goals?

Think about each of these questions, and create a vision of the finished product that you know will satisfy each individual and organization within your total audience. With regard to a Business Plan, that audience typically includes, but is not limited to:

- City/Town Planning Board, Zoning Board, City Council
- License and Permit Issuing Agencies
- Senior Bank Loan Officer/Loan Review Board
- Private Investors
- Prospective Business Partners
- Lawmakers
- Boards of Directors
- Grant/Other Funding Review Boards
- Management Teams and Employees
- Community Leaders

As you can see, the reading audience for a Business Plan will often include a variety of people with different interests and needs. So how can you produce a single document that will satisfy everyone?

The Executive Summary will satisfy some readers. The narrative built into the body of each chapter will satisfy others. The supporting documentation in the appendices will answer more in-depth questions. The table of contents itself allows each reader to focus on a particular area of interest. Bankers and creditors may be most interested in the financial section. License- and permit-issuing agencies may be most interested in the location and layout aspects of your business, and so on.

The tables of contents available to you may or may not fill your needs. Do not hesitate to add chapters or sections as appropriate. **Having now considered your total reading audience, and ensuring that a complete set of topical contents is in place, you need to focus now on the <u>order</u> of the presentation-- that is, its organization and flow.**

What is the best sequence for your table of contents and presentation? Which topical order will result in the smoothest read for your audience? Is it best to address your major obstacles or challenges early on or later in the document?

Take the time to play around with different organizations. Seek advice from others, and rearrange the order until you come up with the one that is best for you. There are no hard and fast rules when it comes to ordering topics in your Business Plan.

Our next consideration is the <u>tone</u> of your writing. Is your writing formal or informal? What mood should your writing express? Is it powerful and persuasive? Tone is the voice and emotion in your written words.

Within the context of a Business Plan, key terms might include profit maximization, environmentally friendly, community tax base, job creation, untapped markets, top quality, and safety. It's easy to see how these words might appeal to your banker, local planning board member, or public safety officer.

As you prepare and send your Business Plan to key people, is it best to use their first name, last name, or formal job title? Should a short note or memo be typed or hand-written? How formal your writing should be depends on the relationship and rapport that you have with each person or company.

How technically knowledgeable is your audience? Be sure to communicate clearly.

Removing a reader's known objections, questions and concerns, are written components of persuasion. If your banker is worried about the cash flow aspects of your venture and your ability to repay the loan, you must present a persuasive narrative that will make those fears go away.

Always put yourself in the reader's shoes before communicating.

The final step leading to the creation of your first draft is the pre-writing or outline stage. Create an outline of some sort-- <u>something in writing</u> that you will use to create that first draft. You may choose a standard outline, or a stack of 3x5 cards with key words and notes, or perhaps a flow chart with headings and subheadings. Use what works best for you, but use something. **Be sure to consider the three main components--content, order, and tone.**

It's time to write. Move quickly through the writing of your first draft. **Trust your outline and keep moving.** Do not stop or get hung up on details. A first draft is, after all, just a first draft. You're looking only for something to work with.

All major revisions in content and order typically occur between the first and second drafts. So at this point, first draft in hand, your editing eye is focused on getting the final structure in place.

All subsequent edits focus primarily on the presentation aspects of appearance, spelling, grammar, and ease of readability. Now may be the time to bring other people back into the process. It is always beneficial to have another set of eyes critique your written work, regardless of how well you write.

Those of you who are weak writers must bring other people into the editing process. Everyone seems to know someone who writes well and at this point there is nothing wrong with getting some editing help.

In the real world, I have seen many prospective business owners and entrepreneurs wisely solicit editing help from the very people and organizations who would ultimately approve or deny their application for funding, licenses, permits, and so on.

You must edit for perfection. Misspellings and grammatical errors are unprofessional and cost you credibility. They distract the reader from your main points.

As important as it is for you to fine-tune your presentation and eliminate errors, you must still know when to say when. Editing can drive you crazy and go on forever. It is (arguably) humanly impossible to catch every error. We are after all, business people, not English professors.

With the content set and the editing completed, now consider appearance and audience analysis as it pertains to presentation.

Considerations in how to best present your Business Plan may include but are not limited to:

- Title/Cover Page and Binder
- Color and Style of Paper
- Computer Graphics, Charts, Pictures, Spreadsheets
- Section Markers and Dividers
- Video Attachments
- Appendices and Supporting Documentation (Data, Maps, References)

It is worth spending a few dollars at your local copy center.

Congratulations. You have successfully completed a long and tedious process and have produced a fine document. This can and will pay off for you many times throughout your career in many ways.